# The Corporate Thug

## Table of Contents

- *i.*     Dedication
- *ii.*    Foreword
- *iii.*   Preface
- *iv.*   Poetic Reflections of an Intelligent Thug's Passion
  - *i.*     The Corporate Thug
  - *ii.*    The Purse Snatcher
  - *iii.*   I.D. Check
  - *iv.*   Suck It Up
  - *v.*     The Attached Glot
  - *vi.*   He's My Honey of an O"
  - *vii.*   Step Daddy
  - *viii.* Same Chic Different Day
  - *ix.*   I Popped Rocked His Ass
  - *x.*     The Church Man
  - *xi.*   Temptation
  - *xii.*   The Confused Man
  - *xiii.* Why Commit
  - *xiv.* Igniting the Purse
  - *xv.*   Stalker Tendencies
  - *xvi.* Conveniently Stroking
  - *xvii.* It's Never Yours; It's Just Your Time
  - *xviii.* Dress Shoes or Timbs
  - *xix.* Sassy Yet Classy
  - *xx.*   Enough with the Guessing!
  - *xxi.* I'm Your Father, Not Your Friend
- *v.*     Acknowledgements

## **Dedication**

*This book is dedicated to GOD as he created man in the simplest form that women just don't understand!*

*This book is dedicated to the woman that gave me life; and the courage she instilled to think I could do this twice!*

*This book is dedicated to the fliest guy! And for those who are unsure, My SON'S the apple of my eye!*

*This book is dedicated to men that are simply confused by women, their complexity and all of their rules!*

*This book is dedicated to my two ANGELS GOD called home in 2008. Wish you were here ladies to share and celebrate!*

*This book is dedicated to my grandmother, who was affectionately known as "my girl," who always told me I was beautiful in such a complex world!*

*This book is dedicated to the analytical girl, whose thoughts have kept her enjoying life in the SINGLE WORLD!*

*Lastly, this book is dedicated to all who will inquire. I thank you, be blessed, and I hope you're INSPIRED!*

# Foreword

*It is with honor and a great deal of pride that I am so close to a star that shines so bright. Arshima "Alluring" Davenport holds numerous titles: mother, daughter, granddaughter, niece, aunt, sister, vocalist, president, supervisor, dear friend, poet, scholar and woman of God. She initially embarked upon a new and exciting chapter in her life in 2013, when she birthed her first book "My Purse Comes First". She has always had a way with words and could engage anyone in conversation as she exuberates an inviting and kinship spirit to anyone she encounters. As for me, I represent that which keeps her focused and confident about who she is and whose she is. It is apparent that she is aware that with God all things are possible as she fearlessly goes after anything she wants with the expectation that it will happen! This is a reflection of God continuously showering her with His favor.*

*Now to some the poetry that is written may seem a bit "risky". Some may wonder why she would want to even give a poetic voice to this type of content that is so private and unmentionable to some. Sometimes it's the silent voice that needs to be heard; someone may need to know what it takes to please their mate or they are not getting the response they are accustomed to. This poetry deals with real life. Some who read it will relate or reminisce, some will stop and ponder if they are the woman this man is speaking of, others will find this as confirmation of what they've been feeling, while others may reflect and realize a change that has to be made. Whatever the emotion, please know that these poems represent the reality that some man or woman deal with every day. So don't critique this book based on the implied erotic content. Instead, celebrate with me the gift of the author and her creativity in giving "intimate desires" new life!*

*A standing ovation is order as there is no one prouder of your accomplishments, not only as poet and author, but all of the many hats you wear so well. May God bless you and guide your footsteps as you continue to walk in His blessings.*

# *Preface*

This book is the spin-off from "My Purse Comes First", which was written after a girl's night out with my dearest friends and family. The poems and evening were supposed to be that of fun and a little classy "bad girl" behavior. The book was a great success to the point that men were requesting more copies than women as it helped them to better understand us. I guess we were telling all the secrets that men were challenged with in relationships. As a result of this, every day for the past three years I have been asked to write another book. I wondered what I would title it or if I wanted to accomplish this a second time. I then began to reflect back on how many men used the first book to gain their own personal knowledge of how to interact with women. I thought how unfair this would be to women if I didn't afford them the same opportunity, so I did. I began to interview men that were close to me and engaged them in conversations that would help develop my material. I also engaged those regarding titles and asked them to expound upon their opinions and views. The men loved the interaction and some even were so aroused by their own thoughts that they included pictures

## The Corporate Thug

with their submissions. So often we as women say that men just don't understand or they just don't get it! We find ourselves frustrated by this because we really don't have a clue as to why they act in this manner. The truth of the matter is they are not acting, but their thought process and mindset is just not complicated and we are! All men want to know is what we want in the simplest terms and they will oblige our requests. All of the extra thought and emotion that we require and expect them to understand is what creates the issues. So, women take all of your complexities and analytical skills and use them to dissect the material in this book to help clarify what men want and need! I guarantee that you will find yourself or your relationship in this book. Now sit back, relax, grab a glass of wine and a notepad as you are about to experience being swept off your feet by **THE CORPORATE THUG!**

## *Opening to the Corporate Thug*

*This man is one that wins all the women over! He looks good, smells good, is fashionable, and intelligent. He doesn't even have to sell himself because he is a visual stimulant! Women need to be careful with this man or they may find themselves with their panties in his hands!*

## The Corporate Thug

So confident in his walk with style you admire; he knows he's the prospect for hire!

He gives a slight smile careful not to flirt, but his intent all along is to get under your skirt!

You're so flattered you've finally caught his eye, but the truth of the matter is you didn't even have to try!

See you were already prey unbeknown to you; he was already contemplating on how to pursue!

So he greets you daily as if it's innocent; this is all to disguise his true intent!

He's polite, intelligent and facilitates meetings with ease! With a talk game so strong he weakens your knees!

Smooth operator huh? Subliminal seduction; now your purse is experiencing potential eruption!

You've been baited and now he's reeling you in, but are you skilled enough to contend?

Are you mentally prepared for his delivery? Or will be as a guarded knight awaiting medieval chivalry!

# The Corporate Thug

*Be careful with the man whose talk game is on point; he'll use that same tongue and your purse he'll anoint!*

*You'll feel sedated and in a slight trance as a result of how you're being romanced!*

*Your purse in awe as she constantly sheds tears and shows no remorse for clogging his ears!*

*You may experience lower back pain or your waist being sore; as a result of positions never experienced before!*

*Complaints don't exist; your purse has never been more satisfied!! And the purses ability to resist has been denied!*

*So if you're feeling faint as if you've been drugged; these are just side effects from your encounter with the* **Corporate Thug!!**

## The Corporate Thug

# *Intro to the Purse Snatcher*

*This man seductively persuades women by being suave. He is very polite, but deliberate with his intent! He knows what he wants from any woman and has a strategy to get it. Looking anxious or desperate is never an option, but gaining what he wants is! He lures one in by his mental stimulation, class and style then before you know it; the purse has been snatched!*

# The Purse Snatcher

*Seductively walking as you stroll through my mind; the visual I replay is watching you from behind!*

*Daily I wonder just how it would feel to enter a purse so tightly sealed!*

*We pass in the hall, innocently she smiles when I speak; while all I can imagine is making her purse leak!*

*So being the man that I am I begun to strategize on what it would take to wear her inner thighs!*

*Around my waist and my face, there's no limit to what I'll do; and to ensure I lose no traction, oh yeah I'm keeping on my shoes!*

*She drinks specialty coffee always hot, never chilled, so midday I make an offer to get her a refill!*

*Surprised by the offer and appreciative of the gesture; I become quite anxious, but mustn't crack under pressure!*

*The pressure I'm speaking is my anatomy growing against my zipper, due to the sexiness of her voice as she shows gratitude when her coffee's delivered.*

*She stated "this coffee tastes almost as good as I do"! The opening I've been waiting for, she has no clue!*

*I reply "that's interesting and what's your flavor"? My taste buds are so broad, I'm sure I will savor!*

## The Corporate Thug

*So, I take her to dinner, Surf and turf she enjoyed; a little red wine to ensure this check isn't returned void!*

*We go back to her place as I've set the tone and I play some soft music via my Cell Phone!*

*She unwound and relaxed the more we conversed; then moistened my ruler straddling me with her purse!*

*She was everything I imagined and a really good "catcher"; Mission accomplished, she's been abducted by **"The Purse Snatcher"**!*

## *Exordium to I.D. Check*

*This man tries to overcompensate for his shortcomings! He has a great career and provides her with everything a women needs emotionally while providing stability. There is just one thing that's really strange; every time the topic of intimacy arises he becomes uncomfortable! He becomes busy and makes excuses why he can't. Be careful of this type of man as you may be in for an unexpected surprise!*

## The Corporate Thug

# *I.D. Check*

*He comes across arrogant and full of pride, so you never know what he's carrying inside.*

*Better yet the lack there of, which is why he's so vocal. His strategy is to make you less focal!*

*He tries to over compensate for where he falls" short", so he sells you dreams of how he'll support!*

*You become intrigued and the lifestyle seems ideal; not knowing his secret could break the deal!*

*Over time you become closer and of each other grow fonder, so naturally your mind begins to wonder!*

*Why hasn't he ever tried to be intimate with me? Maybe I need see if he has an I.D.!*

*See I.D. is short for "Infant Dick" and prayerfully you don't find that you've been tricked!*

*You suggest an evening of passionate events, but notice whenever mentioned he becomes quite tense!*

*He makes excuses like he's tired or working late, but your purse is impatient due to the need to relate!*

# The Corporate Thug

*Finally, you agree and schedule a date! And your purse is anxious from the long wait!!*

*The foreplay is unbelievable as you reached new highs, but you notice in his pants there is no "rise"!*

*You ask yourself is something wrong with me? So you step up your game and drop to your knees!*

*Oh my goodness!! Is something wrong with my eyes? Was all the proclaimed success just a disguise?*

*How old is this man? He looks like he's two? I should have paid more attention to the size of his shoe!*

*Fortunately, he's fine and financially fit, which is the only reason you opt not to split!*

*So ladies to prevent a sexual wreck; do yourself a favor and perform an **I.D. Check!***

## Prelude to "Suck it Up"

Women always say what they are not going to do and expect men to just accept it. Men are expected to remain interested and not want more from women sexually! Yes, women carry the prize, but it's important they know that "women" is plural, so what one woman will not do, the next one will, so get On-board! After all, women want it all, so why not give us the same? Continue saying what you will not do and remember that at some point men get tired of hearing that and will get what they want even if it's not from you!

# The Corporate Thug

## *Suck It Up*

Special occasions only is what you say, but you want me to taste you every other day!

What's wrong with this picture; I mean is it me? Am I just here to serve with no satisfaction to me?

Oh you say you're a vegetarian and don't eat meat, but I need a carnivore to be in my sheets!

See in the beginning you were all in; now you feed me bull like it depends!

**I need a woman willing to please from all aspects and not sitting around worrying if I'll lose respect!**

The respect is loss as you play too many games; and I find your excuses to be quite lame!

So adhere or let it roll off your back like a duck, but my suggestion is you learn to suck it up!!!

## *Intro to the Attached Glot*

This man desires a relationship more than just to hit it and quit it. He wants someone that he can relate to on a deeper level than just sex. He wants to learn and feel her on another level. He's looking to see if this woman is wife material and not just wasting his time. Women say this is what they want, but are so accustomed to not getting this from a man they often time don't know how to receive it. They are also afraid to admit that this is what they want in fear that what they are reading from the man is not what the same. Ladies, if this is what the man is saying, then take it at face value because a man will not say anything he does not mean!

## The Attached Glot

*Most pistols are used to shoot and kill; this pistol is used to create thrills!*

*Many pistol carriers are locked and loaded; waiting for the right woman that can hold it!*

*This gun is a little different; target practice is not my goal! This time I'm aiming for the mate to my soul!*

*No longer do I want to just aim and shoot, but rather learn and earn and develop a root!*

*See roots are the foundation of anything that grows, so it's important they're strong if you plan to uphold!*

*This pistol wants more than being inserted into your holster; let's wine, dine and become mentally closer!*

*Now don't get it confused I still aim to please; and will always enjoy a woman on her knees!*

*I'm just trying to change from being a male that explores; in fear I may be missing out on having more!*

*I want to experience love and being attached at the hip; as we take the world by storm in admiration of our partnership!*

## The Corporate Thug

*I'm ready to move forward and start a new life; no longer looking to create shooting victims, but now a wife!*

*So if you feel you would be a good catch; just remember this* ***Glot*** *has strings attached!!*

# Opening to I'm Her Honey Of an "O"

*This was just a cute poem written while eating my favorite breakfast! The mood was great and the sensation felt as I swallowed the oats sent my mind into a whirlwind as my purse began to spin! Now, it's important to remember that breakfast can be served and enjoyed at any time of the day, so don't limit yourself to early morning's. Breakfast is whenever he "rises" or she "rains"! Men love to experience breakfast at anytime. The recipient of this meal in the lucky one!*

## The Corporate Thug

# *I'm Her Honey of an "O"*

*Her bowl is cold and my spoon is chilled; awaiting to give her this honey of an o refill!*

*See it's no question that we'll repeat, as her purse gets warmer and starts to leak!!*

*The combination of her honey combining with my oats; makes my soul happy as I coat her throat!*

*On the dining room table or the kitchen sink; she's ready anytime all I have to do is wink!*

*Breakfast time in my house is whenever I "rise", and she's always ready as her my purse moistens her thighs!*

**Protein is a great way to get her energy flowing; and once my tongue touches her purse, she not only rains, she's snowing!**

*The wholesomeness of my oats she'll experience once I release; keeps her skin forever pretty and her mind at peace!*

*Great tasting and healthy and right under her nose; She's fallen in love with my Honey of an O!*

## *Exordium to Step-daddy*

A man that can step in and take the place of an absent father is amazing! Often time's women have to wear multiple hats, so when they get a man that steps in and steps up, it's appreciated! The key here is that the woman has to put it down from the start. She has to show that she is about her business from all aspects. Men are visual, so once he sees this, it's an automatic turn on! Just watch how this man falls in line and gives what she needs because all men want to feel needed and appreciated. He just needs to know the woman's efforts are sincere!

## The Corporate Thug

# *Step-daddy*

Working hard daily at completing her requests; overcompensating to avoid undue stress!

See in dating her I acquired a package deal; she needed a real man and not an intermittent thrill!

As a single woman, trying to raise a young man is tough; he needs a strong example and someone he can trust!

Oh I can't deny this woman is tight; she keeps her hair, nails, and definitely that body right!

My rapport with her son keeps her pleased and she thanks me frequently on her knees!

She knows exactly how to get to a man's heart and orally greeting my manhood is a great start!

Many see the term step-daddy as being the worse, but they don't know the power of her purse!

She freaks me from high to low; so mind blowing, she curls my toes!

My mind she soothes, my body she holds; when she's done my release I can't control!

So continue gossiping or just being chatty as I continue to take pride enjoying all the perks of being step-daddy!

# *Prelude to Same Chic Different Day*

Men love spontaneity and variety in their relationships. This doesn't mean they want to add additional people, but rather their woman needs to be open to different options and creativity in the bedroom! Keeping him anxious and curious keeps him coming home! Ladies DO NOT get comfortable with doing the same thing the same way all the time. Men will continue to receive what you have to offer, but the minute someone offers them something different, it becomes very appealing to them. Keep your man interested and what others have to offer will not even be a factor!

## *The Corporate Thug*

# *Same Chic Different Day*

*Relationships can become real predictable, which causes him to sometimes be despicable!*

*Never with the intent to hurt his girl, but this new experience is a different world!*

*See when he walks through the door, she's ready without delay as she orally greets him, then asks about his day.*

*She understands her role and that's to relieve his stress, so she begins implementing new tests!*

*There are days when he walks in and she'll be his maid, dust him off, clean him up, then pour a glass of lemonade!*

*Sometimes she's the plumber aka Mrs. Draino because she understands her job, which is to keep his sack low!*

*She's even played homeless, which blew his mind! Especially, when she was naked and he read the sign! "NO monetary donations, I work for free; nuts and screws are all that's needed to please me!"*

*She's creative, spontaneous and willing to do new things; then he comes home and is greeted by plain Jane?!*

*He'll show what he likes without saying a word, so this is your time to mentally observe!*

*Be es-tut and ensure you take good notes; then work him over from the book you wrote!*

*Make him wonder if this is what he's been missing, simply by your ability to pay sexual attention!*

*Missionaries are servants and aim to please, so don't be afraid to bring him to his knees!*

# The Corporate Thug

*Now, this has become a partnership, so don't sell yourself short, but maintain your grip and his shoulders for your support!*

*Ensure that you to, are sent into outer space, so take pleasure in moisturizing his face!*

*Send him off unable to wait until he can return! You've ignited the fire again, Burn Baby Burn!*

*Now all he thinks about is how you're lickable, but never again will he call you **PREDICTABLE!***

# Preface to I Popped Rock His Ass

*Doing the same things all the time becomes boring! Not only for men, but women as well! Men want to experience something different at times that would make their toes curl and their eyes rollback in their head. Men are even more intrigued when the woman initiates the change. Although men like to be in control, they also like to be surprised and controlled intimately! They like women to be aggressive as long as they are being pleased. They will participate in the role play even if they say they won't because they want so much to reach a new level with you. Something **NEW** is your biggest **CLUE!***

## The Corporate Thug

# *I Pop Rocked His Ass*

*Sitting on the bed talking trash; And before he knew it, I Pop Rocked His Ass!*

*Stripped him down to only his wife beater and socks, then prepped my mouth with watermelon Pop Rocks!*

*The Fizzle he hears makes his stomach quiver, but the sensation he feels makes his anatomy shiver!*

*Wh wh what is this he stutters, trying to maintain his composure, but he's putty in my hands; I'm controlling his soldier!*

*See he's standing at attention waiting to fire off at the mouth; attribute this to the oral stimulation she performed down south!*

*He's accustomed to leading, but now he must follow; as she's now in control and remember she swallows!*

*Now you're afraid of what you're feeling inside and your testosterone helps you hold on to your pride!*

*Being the woman I am, I'll give him this pass, but he'll never forget who Pop Rocked his Ass!*

# *Preface to the Church Man*

*Men know that all women love a man that's God fearing. A man that loves God is supposed to know how to love a woman. Men know this, so going to church has always been a great way to meet and interact with various women. Women need to be careful with this man and ensure his intentions are good. No woman wants to be caught by this church man, so it's important that women carry themselves in a respectful and upright manner or they will become his next victim!*

## The Church Man

*Attending church every Sunday punctual and well dressed; knowing I send the women into distress!*

*God fearing and handsome, what a powerful combination; with this trump card here I get plenty of relations!*

*The funny thing is I relax and they approach, which contradicts the teaching of our spiritual coach!*

*The offers are fruitful as they multiply in numbers, so I inspect the purses of the female members!*

*Some Say I'm hell bound and labels me the worst, but what they forget is that I'm a man first!*

*Now, I could see if I were soliciting, but that's not the case; they're outright offering their purses at an alarming pace!*

*They always start by saying they're waiting for their king, but have no problem showing me their G-String!*

*So, am I wrong for obliging their request and relieving their purse of its sexual distress?*

*I simply give them what they want and best believe I deliver; acting as if you're in the spirit when that purse begins to shiver!*

*For some this may be hard to believe and that's probably because your purse is being relieved!*

## *The Corporate Thug*

*But, this group of ladies has been on a drought, so I'm willingly helping the sistas out!*

*So, ladies please be careful if this is not in your plan; or you may find your purse under the influence of the* **Church Man!**

## *Exordium to Why Commit*

So often women think they can win a man over by giving him everything. They give him unlimited sex, cook, clean, and reside with him just as his girlfriend. They are giving the man everything he wants and needs without him committing, so why would he? Women in order to get different results you have to make demands and change your strategy!

# The Corporate Thug

## *Why Commit*

*Day after day the same routine, you wake me, relate to me then prepare my cuisine!*

*Now, I'm not complaining, the treatment is inspiring; to the point where we have conversations of retiring!*

*But that's the extent, I'm all talk no action;* **I mean why should I? I'm still receiving free satisfaction!**

*I walk in from work there's hot food on the stove; I take a shower and you hand me my robe!*

*Family functions come around and you already have gifts and if someone needs a ride you give them a lift!*

*You treat my children as if they're your own; doing homework, attending functions and always calling on the phone!*

*When my boys come over you're well behaved as we chill in the comforts of my "man cave"!*

*If I've had a rough day and work has disturbed my peace; you orally restore it by helping me release!*

*Now, being the man that I am, I make sure you're pleased as I wipe off your face then drop to my knees!*

*I arch you against the wall as you close your eyes and use my shoulders to support your thighs!*

*This purse is so sweet it could cause decay, but I wouldn't have my face moistened any other way!*

# The Corporate Thug

*Advanced perks like a spouse I must admit, but all of this with no "titles",* **WHY WOULD I COMMIT?!**

## *Prelude to Temptation*

No matter how great the relationship is men are always tempted! It has nothing to do with what a woman is or is not doing. It is just in a man's nature to want to try something new, especially when it's real "eye candy"! The dangerous part is when the woman carries it nonchalantly and the man feels ignored. Once this happens is Game Time!

# *Temptation*

*I see you every morning rushing to your car; stylish and flashy looking like a superstar!*

*You make beauty look easy and with a personality to match; I could see how any man would grow attached!*

*Even on weekends your relaxed look is sweet; Nice fitting sweat suit with "J's" on your feet!*

*Yes, I'm in a relationship, but reside alone and as good as you look, I wanna make you my home!*

*Now, I'm not saying I'm unhappy, so don't get that notion; you just send my body into sexual commotion!*

*The way your body moves with each stride you take; even when I'm alone with my palms I relate!*

*I love my girl, she was all I could see, but it's something about you that keeps tugging at me!*

*I know what is, you play it cool while I'm losing my mind acting a plum fool!*

*You're so nonchalant and not even pressed, which is really what has me so stressed!*

*Oh No, this is not supposed to happen this way; gotta switch this up, now you're my prey!*

*I'll pay less attention in passing, she'll see; then she'll begin to wonder what's wrong with me!*

*Now she becomes even more exposed; the warmer it gets the lesser her clothes!*

## *The Corporate Thug*

*It's been a month and still no response and I find a note in my mailbox!*

*Hey stranger, it's your neighbor, what's up with you? Maybe we can converse over a drink or two!*

*Now, the tables have turned, let the games begin; I'll convert her into my sexual friend!*

*The more she drank the looser she became; if I take it right now it'll be such a shame!*

*I'll just be the gentlemen and take her home, tuck her in then call her phone!*

*Checkmate, I got her, now I'll make my move; allow her to come over and play it smooth!*

*She arrives at my door offering to cleanse my face and I send her purse into outer of space!*

*The feelings we exchanged were of extreme sensation; we've both fallen victim of sexual* **Temptation!**

## *Intro to Igniting the Purse*

*Ninety percent of sexual intimacy is mental. If you can stimulate her mind before even touching her body, then you've already hit a home-run! Women are emotional creatures and also introverts, so getting into their minds send a message to their body that ignites a sexual energy and explosion beyond the imagination! An ignited purse is one that disburses the heat necessary for a long night of passion. Learn to speak the language of the purse and ignition is automatic!*

## The Corporate Thug

# *Igniting the Purse*

*Feed a man and he'll give you his heart; or does premature sexing earn that prize from the start!*

*As a man our goal is to always sexually please; and of course we'll take a purse given with ease*

*A purse turned on without mental stimulation; makes a man question potential penetration*

*See as a man we're always up for the chase, but it's a turn off when you're throwing your purse in our face!*

*It's a challenge dealing with a purse that's on chill and the intellectual conversation turns my piece into steel!*

*Now it's time to make love to her mind; telling her of the pleasures she'll experience over time!*

*Not only being sexual, but offer stability as well; makes her waters begin to trouble and my ship will sail!*

*But still I refrain from going for the goal; although her body is calling I want to stimulate her soul!*

*The sexual tension is getting heavy, but I choose to wait and our chemistry's so strong, we touch ourselves to relate!*

*It's been three months now and the time has arrived to insert my body between her thighs!*

*I'll plan a relaxing evening and prepare our dinner; then take it slow as if I'm a beginner!*

*Listening to soft jazz while sipping wine; then I'll ask her to dance and start a slow grind!*

*Her knees become weak as her purse becomes wet; anxiously anticipating, she grabs my neck!*

## The Corporate Thug

*I hold her close as she releases a sigh and massage my ear lobes with her inner thigh!*

*As I gently caress her inner walls with my tongue; she's gasping for air to re-expand her lungs!*

*Changing positions, she' now on her face as I'm stroking her purse at a slow steady pace!*

*Her sensual moans sends chills down my spine, as I firmly smack her from behind!*

*She holds me tight as she straddles my lap and the passion of my strokes makes her take a nap!*

*The extreme passion and intimacy was out of sight because when mentally stimulated the purse will **Ignite!***

## Prelude to the Confused Man

A man rarely changes unless there is something in his life requiring him to. Men are normally satisfied with doing the same things daily and being pretty predictable. When a man changes and it's noticeable, that's when the woman's sensors should elevate! Men don't just change up in the middle of something that seems to be going fine unless something has caught their attention. The question is, what's his real focus? I promise you this poem here will throw you for a loop!

## *The Confused Man*

*My body's there when we're together, but my mind's far away; contemplating how to let you know we've reached a new day!*

*See we're that power couple taking the world by storm; and every time they see me, it's you on my arm!*

*And when we get home, I'm very attentive to your needs; you call me, I run; your sexual appetite I feed!*

*We both have great careers that call for crazy hours; now does that explain when I come home why I need to take a shower?*

*I come in extremely anxious with very little to say; I reply while undressing "I'm washing off my day"!*

*She assumes my workday was rough, which is the implied intent; as she has no clue how my day was really spent!*

*She joins me in the shower and massages me from behind; as she feels the need to orally help me unwind!*

*Now, usually this would ignite an immediate erection; as he's always prepared for purse affection!*

*But not this time to her surprise; and you could see the concern within her eyes!*
*She begins to question what's wrong with me and I tell I her I need to be more free!*

# The Corporate Thug

*Not from her, but to be more open; as she's not the only one I've been stroken!*

*So I tell her of my desires, which includes more variety and I want her support in its entirety!*

*I don't want her to feel inadequate in anyway, but I'm struggling with whether I'm straight or gay!*

*See she consoles and comforts me from a woman's perspective; but he manhandles me, and then holds me, almost overprotective!*

*He understands the everyday struggles of a man; where she doesn't understand why talking isn't always in the plan!*

*There are times as soon I hit the door; he cuffs me, stuffs me and shoves my face to the door!*

*He doesn't need to converse, actions speaks louder than words; the sighs of passion and relief are all that's heard!*

*Now, she makes love making awesome as her purse makes me spazz; and she scats on my mic like raw jazz!*

*I have the best of both worlds and don't even care; due to the life I'm living, I dare to share!*

*Some may feel I'm selfish because they don't understand, but those that do, know why I'm a* **CONFUSED MAN!**

## *Intro to Stalker Tendencies*

*If every time you go someplace she shows up you should be concerned. If anytime your phone rings or there is a notification, it's her, then you should be concerned. Men need their space and also the need to be trusted. This means if they say they are going out, don't ask where, don't ask who they are talking to, nor clock their whereabouts. A sure way to lose a man is smothering him outside of the bedroom! Let him breathe!*

## Stalker Tendencies

Man I should have followed all the clues; I knew once I hit it she'd act a fool!

She calls back to back when I don't reply; when asked her reasoning she doesn't know why!

When I'm working she constantly texts and if I don't respond the parking lot's next!

I tell her I'm going to church in hopes of finding peace; I receive a text saying look behind you three seats!

We talk after church and she asks of my plans; I tell her to watch the games with my man.

Never mentioned where, so I thought I was good, so why is the chic in the bar wearing a hood?!

She even starts social media wars; then when she loses the battle, she bangs on my door!

I guess I should have kept it platonic; because this girl acts like she is hooked on phonics!

Maybe it was the slow stroke that's impacting her mind; should I have rushed and not taken my time?

Or was it the spontaneity of sexing in the car; that interaction alone may have taken her too far!

Could it have been going to New York by train; when I rode her caboose and made her purse rain!

I think it was how we lit Lady Liberty's torch; or how I handled her purse in the swing on the porch!

Keeping it traditional may have kept her calm as she's now meeting with Psychics to read her palms!

Psychics I'm lost, really what's her goal; she says she feels I'm the mate for her soul!

Now I'm feeling pressure and she needs to chill; this is not a relationship I care to build!

# The Corporate Thug

*As a man I move at my own pace; I'm entitled to have my own personal space!*

*So cutting her off seems to be the only remedy; as she's proven to have real **STALKER TENDENCIES!***

## *Opening to Conveniently Stroking*

*This woman knows her role in a man's life. She doesn't expect a relationship because she doesn't want the commitment. She's there to please and to be pleased. Late night is her preference because she doesn't want everyone to see you coming or going. She's always ready and there is no limit to what she will do! This is where a man can be free to be himself and free of strings! Each time you all encounter each other the experience reaches new heights. She is what every man wants at home, but once a chic becomes the "one" these actions are no longer received. With that being said, until a man is tired and decides to settle down, she is a player's dream!*

# The Corporate Thug

## *Conveniently Stroking*

*As we all know convenience stores are open 24 hours; this purse shares its similarity and knows its power!*

*She has everything you need and her rack is stacked; as they stare me in my face as she lies on her back!*

*I call at 2 A.M. and she asks for my order; I request the massage of her lips after a glass of warm water!*

*She says although it's late you don't have to settle for snacks; I want to ensure pure satisfaction, so let's go for the max!*

*See I understand my role and I aim to please, so I'll start by licking your toes, then the backs of your knees!*

*I want to hit spots that will make you moan; as you're now in overdrive and that's the most powerful zone!*

*I'll make you reach all kinds of highs; while my tonsils are tickled while massaging your thighs!*

*Now I'll move to your chest so muscular it's rippled as I use my tongue to massage your nipples!*

*At attention you're standing and I'll make you salute while assisting with putting on your rain suit!*

*See this mission is accomplished with no strings attached, so it's imperative to ensure NO eggs are hatched!*

## The Corporate Thug

*I'll straddle you slowly taking my time, then swerve and curve, now we're stroking from behind!*

*I then position my body as if I'm in a Cocoon as you follow my lead and become my human spoon!*

*Now I'll follow your lead as I'm completely exposed; as my headboard is tapped by the tips of my toes!*

*The thrill is so high we explode together; as your rain suit was proper attire for this weather!*

*Even at 2 A.M. your options are wide open; thus clarifies the meaning of **CONVENIENTLY STROKING!***

## Prelude to "It's Never Yours; It's Just Your Time"

Men always want to feel like they own the purse. They ask questions and perform sexual acts that stroke their ego! The funny thing is women will say what you want to hear in a time of intimacy and if you are in a relationship. Now think about it, do you think that the man before you didn't ask the same questions? Don't you think he wanted his ego stroked as well? Of course he does! So let's be real men, when we're in a relationship with a woman; keep in mind that whoever a woman is in a relationship with, she will make them feel the SAME WAY!

## *It's Never Yours; It's Just Your Time*

*No matter the time, not matter the place constant satisfaction displays on your face!*

*On the tabletop or on the floor even in the quiet room at the bookstore!*

*Riding down the street 50 miles per hour my mic is awakened with her oral power!*

*Movie theatres are easy; we have them on lock bending her over the seat with a slow steady rock!*

*Flying out of town is always the best; christening the walls of the lavatory while others rest!*

*Not to mention, when we go to the beach; rocking the lifeguard stand while out of reach!*

*NBA games, way up in the stands, I please her purse with the touch of my hand!*

*Now a nice warm shower always warms the stove; then I bend her over to touch her toes!*

*We're so spontaneous, it happens anywhere; hallways, exits even the emergency stairs!*

*So, with all this being said you would think it's mine, but fellas **IT'S NEVER YOURS; IT'S JUST YOUR TIME!***

# Exordium to Introduction to Dress Shoes or Timbs

*Many think that men's shoes are only for the purpose of the walking, but that is far from the truth! Shoes have multiple purposes in a relationship, especially when it comes to intimacy. As a man you want to always please a woman to the best of your ability. In doing so you have to know the type of woman you are dealing with and if your actions with require traction or not! Is she that chic that likes it rough, so you need to keep your balance or is she that subtle chic that likes it slow and easy? Knowing this in advance helps the man properly prepare for a performance beyond measure.*

## The Corporate Thug

# *Dress Shoes or Timbs*

*They say you can tell a lot about a man by his feet; some are conservative, bold or small and sleek!*

*Now women often times want to know the size as this is a myth that leads to disappointment and lies!*

*See a real man knows how to play the game; as it's not the size, but the shoe determines his fame!*

*Depending on the woman determines the position and whether my feet need traction to complete the mission!*

*See some women like it sensual, so I take my time and dress shoes are suitable while licking her from behind!*

*Taking it nice and slow I can go for miles and I know I've met her approval by the way she smiles!*

*I make her purse feel good while under sneak attack; as I feel the pressure of her nails across my back!*

*Now while this lady's sweet, they're some that want more; like being served on the kitchen table or even the floor!*

*So with this lady I'll go out on a Limb; as the work I'll put in will require my Timbs!*

*Her purse is accustomed to hardcore interaction; so these Timbs will provide the required traction!*

*There is no carpet and these floors are wood, so I must gain leverage to stroke her good!*

# The Corporate Thug

*Posting her up against the wall is no easy job; as control is maintained by my shoes and the door knob!*

*Who cares what the neighbors say as our bodies are revealed while groping her loins in the window seal!*

*Her flavor I savor as my taste buds are fed and I enjoy her every drop from the edge of the bed!*

*In the bathroom propped up on the sink; as she floods on my ship I began to drink!*

*Trying new things makes our arousal even higher; as her purse makes me tremble while being shaken on the dryer!*

*You have to be ready for whatever as things happen on a whim; thus the importance of determining dress shoes or Timbs!*

# Opening to Sassy Yet Classy

*Every man wants a woman who is intelligent and beautiful. He wants her to be versatile enough to facilitate a corporate meeting, but submissive enough to please her man at home! She's not worried about if her man sees her as a freak because she knows that's what he wants. She assures him and ensures that he understands that her freakiness is only for him and will not be shared with others! A little Sass has never hurt anyone as long as she's classy when doing so! This is a sure way to turn a man on and keep him Hot!*

# The Corporate Thug

## Sassy yet Classy

*All men say they don't want a freak; that doesn't apply to the home, but just the streets!*

*In public we want her to be intelligent, but mild and once we're home become wet and wild!*

*Her tone is very professional over the phone, but in the midst passion those tones become moans!*

*She has a demeanor of power in the business world, then follows my commands like a helpless little girl!*

*When I tell her to bow, she asks how low; as I guide her down preparing to blow!*

*She's only content when she knows I'm relieved, so she straddles this stallion like you wouldn't believe!*

*She does things to my body that I can't deny; if it weren't for my pride I would probably cry!*

*She takes me to levels I never thought I could reach and her oral intake, to some she could teach!*

*Her hair is pretty and she's nice and lean; attributing that to her constant shots of protein!*

## *The Corporate Thug*

*We know the effort women place into beauty, so as a man making a contribution is my duty!*

*While at work her purse has intermittent sensations; as she reflects on the kinkiness of our relations!*

*We have no limits to what we do, but to see her in public you'd have no clue!*
*She's the real reason this relationship will go far, as she graciously converts to my personal porn star!*

*She has so many tricks it's hard to keep track and my mind keeps replaying stroking her from the back!*

*See as a man we always want her to be viewed as classy, but always remember to keep the bedroom **SASSY!***

# *Preface to Enough with the Guessing*

*Having to guess what a woman wants is too much for men. Men are really simple creatures that don't have a lot of time for guessing. If it's something you want to know, just ask! If it's something you want done, just say it! Playing the guessing games will just leave everyone frustrated sexually and emotionally. So, ladies save yourselves the headache and just speak out!*

## Enough with the Guessing

As men we are not Complex, so you can't expect that we know what's next!

You tell us one thing, so we think all is well, then you switch up and we're like what the hell!

I mean we're not psychic, so we can't read your mind, so why not just tell us the first time!

If its sex you desire I can accommodate that request; as a man I can help relieve all your stress!

If its companionship you're seeking I can be that as well, but you have to fess up and come out of your shell!

Because of your past you assume I'm the same, but the truth of the matter is they were all lame!

What you wanted didn't matter as they were all for self, and they used your body to maintain their sexual health!

Now our relationship is suffering due to where they fell short while all I want to do is provide emotional support!

I want to be the one that makes your heart sing and one day become your humble King!

So take this as relationship lesson; men just don't know, so enough with the guessing!

## *Intro to I'm Your Father, Not Your Friend*

*This man initially starts out trying to be cool and have a friendship with his son He later finds out that this is not the best way to go raising a teenager. He doesn't want his son to make the same mistakes he's made, so he opts to take a more strategic route with his son. He realizes that at this stage in his son's life, showing him to be a man is more important than being his friend. This should make all men reflect on their importance in their children's lives.*

## The Corporate Thug

# I'm Your Father, Not Your Friend

*My son and I have an open friendship; we talk about games, girls and even times when I've slipped.*

*I tell him of how to date multiple girls; and even make jokes of rocking their worlds!*

*He's a really intelligent kid with a future so bright, but I teach him how to get cookies then post to see how many likes!*

*He needs to know what it's like growing into a man; and after high school I explained that's where real fun begins!*

*I speak to him in terms that I know he can relate; even at the expense of putting his future at stake!*

*Now of course that's not the intent when I initially approach, but I'm trying to play the role of his father and his life coach!*

*Maybe I should reflect back and take a page from my own book; then help him develop a plan opposite of that I took!*

*Like never losing focus of his future and goals or exposing his hand, keep others on their toes!*

*We can talk about things that I didn't understand like fostering relationships and networking to fulfill his future plans!*

# The Corporate Thug

*I will teach the importance of being a scholar, so when he enters corporate America, white will be the color of his collar!*

*See with this power and strategy women will come, but they will have to offer him more than just fun!*

*He'll understand his worth and the value he holds and not settling for a cute face and small waist asking for red bottom soles!*

*He'll meet someone that's on his same page and when they're together their presence sets the stage!*

*Enjoying the perks of life without wondering "what if" because every day you're living is a spiritual uplift!*

*He's been blessed with God's favor since the beginning of time; and even with his struggles he wins every time!*

*Making a change is imperative and the message I'll send; is that I'm his **FATHER FIRST NOT HIS FRIEND!***

## "Acknowledgements"

To God be the Glory for All He has done. Without HIM, I'm a lost soul seeking existence. HE is my strength and my refuge and His praises will continually be in my mouth. I would also like to thank my mother, who has always believed in me and encouraged me to dream. She has never made me feel like my goals were beyond my ability or creativity and always encouraged me to step out on FAITH. As my cousin would say, "she is my ROCK!" Thanks to my son Breon J. Christmas, Jr. who silently motivates me every day to strive to be better and is also my cover model! I love you baby!!! A special thank you to Michael Anderson, the creative designer of this marvelous book cover!! Your patience was immeasurable throughout this process. Thank you to all of the guys that allowed me to bounce ideas off of them; Darius Stith, Kyle Ellis,

*DeAaron Black and Clarence Harris just to name a few. Lastly, thanks to all my family and many dear friends who have advised and supported me throughout this and the many other chapters in my life. Your love has carried me and I could not have done this a second time without you! Peace and Blessings to you all!!!*

## The Corporate Thug

## ARSHIMA "ALLURING" DAVENPORT

*thecorporatethug1@gmail.com*

*http://www.facebook/Thecorporatethug1*

*https://twitter.com/thecorpthug*

# The Corporate Thug

www.ingramcontent.com/pod-product-compliance
Lightning Source LLC
Chambersburg PA
CBHW050706160426
43194CB00010B/2026